A Beaver's River Goes Soccer Ball

By

Michele Jeanmarie

Based on the Spanish book:

El río de los castores

by

Fernando Martínez Gil

Illustrated by Mochu Fajar Shobaru

A Children's Theatre

This is a work of fiction. All of the characters, names, incidents, organizations, and dialogue in this novel are either the products of the author's imagination or are used fictitiously.

Archway Publishing books may be ordered through booksellers or by contacting:

Archway Publishing
1663 Liberty Drive
Bloomington, IN 47403
www.archwaypublishing.com
844-669-3957

Because of the dynamic nature of the Internet, any web addresses or links contained in this book may have changed since publication and may no longer be valid. The views expressed in this work are solely those of the author and do not necessarily reflect the views of the publisher, and the publisher hereby disclaims any responsibility for them.

Interior Image Credit: Mochu Shobaru

ISBN: 978-1-6657-4750-9 (sc)
978-1-6657-4751-6 (e)

Library of Congress Control Number: 2023913928

Print information available on the last page.

Archway Publishing rev. date: 08/01/2023

Characters:

Narrator

César, the soccer ball

Moi, the beaver

Flower 1

Flower 2

Bear 1

Bear 2

Bear 3

Bear 4

Ma

Dog

Cat

Scene: Rainforest

Introduction

It is night. It is a cool night. It is late. Most are asleep, except those working in the fields. I see men moving about, their arms in a jerky, sawing motion, harassing the tree trunks. I hear scratching. Scritch. Scratch. Scritch. Scratch.

Getting closer, I see them digging grooves into the trunks. Long, semi-winding grooves, like channels. I see a milky, white substance flowing down these grooves. Flowing. Flowing. Flowing, like a flowing river, but down the balk of a tree.

Latex. It is latex. From here, latex comes. Rubber.

I see buckets. I see tubs. Buckets and tubs are propped at the bases of these trees. The latex, or rubber, meander into the buckets, into the tubs.

I hear, "Let's leave them there until the sun comes up. They'll only get all over us, like chewing gum."

The latex solidifies into the shapes of the receptacles. I hear the men returning. I scamper. I see the buckets and tubs removed. I hear, "Now, let's see how much we can get from each bucket. Boys and girls will be so happy for their balls and toys; men and women will be so happy for their purses and shoes;" and I will be so happy for my P448, my good smelling sneakers.

The latex is taken to the city, to the factory and are threaded through a machine to become shoes, handbags, kitchen wares, housewares, toys, car parts, most things.

César, the soccer ball is made this way. He is made of rubber. His shoes are made of rubber. Latex. These days, he sits and ponders. Everything is so desolate, so sad, so melancholic.

For once upon a time, there was a long river, which traversed a massive forest. Its waters were clear and crisp, served as nourishment to an infinite number of forest creatures. Among its forest creatures was a beaver named Moi. It just so happens that Moi, the beaver, played a lot with César, the Soccer Ball. No more is it so, for their friend, the river, is looking gloomy.

César, the Soccer Ball was entertained daily along the shore of this great river. He had a special love for this river, as well as great respect. For some, the river served as entertainment, for others, it served as nourishment, while for others, it served as shelter. For César, the soccer ball it was where he bobbled and floated. For Moi, the beaver, it was the source of all three.

No entertainment.
No nourishment.
No shelter.

To all, this river is known as the Great Big Brother. For some time, now, the Great Big Brother is sullen. It appears ill. Its rambunctious flow carries with it corroded cans, nasty nappies, bobbing bottles, carousing caps, ooey-gooey fluid, trashy trash. The fish, which once swam in it are now floating belly up. Other creatures, which once drank from its waters, now vacillate weakly.

Act 1

This inflicted great sadness in Moi, the beaver and César, the soccer ball, so much so that they resolve to search for the causes that ail their Great Big Brother.

With backpacks on their shoulders and P448 sneakers on their feet, in search of the causes of their Great Big Brother's illness, they take off for a cure. They both leave singing with hopes and determination to save Great Big Brother.

At midday, fatigue falls on them. They eat some fruits from their backpacks and fall asleep upon the landing.

Flower 1: Hey! (With shouts) Get up! You are squishing my most beautiful, delicate roots. Get up! Get up, I said!

César, the soccer ball bounces up and notices a bed of flowers. Moi, the beaver shots up and poses to attack. He attempts to get near them when one of them begins to shout:

Flower 2: Be careful! Not here! Ow! Ow! What a moron! Such brute! Can't you see you are stepping on my roots?

Flower 1: Halt! If you would like to speak to us, say what you will from there! Be still and speak now!

César, the soccer ball becomes so disconcerted of the flowers' awful demeanor. He remains immobile, afraid of stepping on the roots, so it was Moi, the beaver, still in his stance, who speaks.

Moi, the beaver: Okay…; pardon me…I only wished …

Flower 1: We don't care what you wished! If you only wish to say something, back up. Say it now, for our time is precious!

Moi, the beaver: It's just that…it's just that we were in search of a cure for our Great Big Brother. Do you know what may be afflicting him?

Flower 1: Bah! That filthy, disgusting river! Who cares?

César, the soccer ball: Filthy? Disgusting? He is not filthy or disgusting, you, ingrates, you, ungrateful flowers! I am his friend. We are his friends, (pointing to Moi, the beaver), and I will not let you speak of him in that way! (Pauses) It's just that, … it's just that… he is ill.

Flower 1: Fine! If you are his friend, tell him he is to move away from us, as far as he can! He is to move his filthy waters from our most delicate, precious roots.

Flower 2: Indeed! He can ruin us. He may alter our beautiful aroma, and no one will want us.

César, the soccer ball: How can you be so ungrateful? He gives you life and provides you with nourishment. Without him what would become of you? Hah! I would love to see what would become of you without its waters.

César, the soccer ball: (With his P448, César, the soccer ball stomps all the more). You don't even smell as good as my sneakers (as he puffs out his body to smell what he could smell)!

Flower 1: Aargh! How wretched and uncultured you are!

Flower 2: Such impertinence! Who might you think you are to insult us that way?

Flower 1: Look froggy. We get our nourishment from the rain, not from any common river.

Flower 2: Yes! Indeed, from fine and fresh rainwater.

César, the soccer ball: Yet, you stink! You are so ridiculous! (More annoyed than *ever*)

Flower 1: Ridiculous? Such insolence!

César, the soccer ball: Yes! Ridiculous! My P448 sneakers smell better than the lot of you.

Flower 2: So little with such little culture. Hah!

Flower 1: Out of here! (She screams annoyingly).

Moi, the beaver: Well, I hope you grow pale and ugly, you, egocentric flowers! (He said indignantly)

Moi, the beaver stoops down for his backpack and with César, the soccer ball, with their P448, begin to stomp and jump all the better, ignoring where they had been forewarned not to step.

Flower 1: Ow! My roots!... Beast!

Flower 2: Get out of here! My precious and delicate roots! Brute, uneducated, froggy!

César, the soccer ball and Moi, the beaver: Our P448s smell better than you!

No water.
No freshness.
No flora.

Act 2

César, the soccer ball and Moi, the beaver are content when Flowers' voices extinguish behind their backs. They walk and walk, until they could go no more. They lean against a tree. They nap.

The next morning, they begin to walk anew in search of a cure for Great Big Brother. Suddenly, as they turn the curve, before their eyes, they see bears skipping and splashing in the water. Some are rubbing each other. Others are rolling along the bank of the river.

César, the soccer ball: It's Rebrú, the Bear. I now know the culprit responsible for Great Big Brother's illness. So shameful!

(He gets angrier and angrier, as he nears the bears).

Moi, the beaver: Enough! Enough! Enough already! (He screams with all his might).

The bears shut up immediately in unison, unaware of the origin of the screams. They look and look and see no one.

César, the soccer ball climbs up and inclines, and with indignation, he adds: Here! Over here! I am here!

This time, his shouts draw attention. The bears look at him dumbfoundedly, not believing their ears, or their eyes. Suddenly, a chorus of cackling cracks the silence.

César, the soccer ball: What are you laughing at?

Bear 1: Let's get out of here. He will certainly devour us! (Teasingly amusing him).

Once again, there is another cackling of laughter. The bears encircle him, each time, laughing even harder.

César, the soccer ball: You are… you are … are… ingrates! Yes! That's what you are! Miserable ingrates! Look what you have done to the waters of our Great Big Brother.

Bear 2: So, this little chump not only screams at us, but accuses us, as well.

Bear 3: Look, you cuckoo-head. It's been years we have been playing with Great Big Brother, and he has never complained.

Bear 4: And if you look yonder, you will see the waters are already dirty. We are not the ones to afflict Great Big Brother.

Beaver bawls uncontrollably. Moi, the beaver follows. The bears console the little chumps.

Bear 4: We, too, feel for Great Big Brother. He is the fountain of life. Without him, we will extinguish.

Bear 1: But … what brings you here?

César, the soccer ball: What do you think brings us here? … We are searching for a cure for Great Big Brother.

Bear 2: And why didn't you tell us?

César, the soccer ball: We did, but you are so filled with yourselves, you did not pause to listen.

Bears: It is Ma!

César, the soccer ball: Ma? Ma? Who is Ma?

Bear 3: Look. Go see. (He points further up the river).

Bear 2: Yes! Go see!

So, César, the soccer ball and Moi, the beaver, in their P448 sneakers, amble along. They bid farewell, heads down, and continue.

No H2O.
No fauna.
No playing.

Act 3

Ma appears from the thickness of the forest. Moi, the beaver stoops down. César, the soccer ball hides behind a rock. Trees are scarce. César, the soccer ball sees many more Ma appear. They see some driving heavy machinery. They see magnificent trees falling. They see other Ma eating, drinking and piling up non-consumables aside.

Moi, the beaver bobs his head around. César, the soccer ball pierces closer.

Who are these creatures? What are they doing. Why are they felling trees? (They ask each other).

Then, appear Dog and Cat.

César, the soccer ball: Psst … Hey! (Although in a whisper, he attempts to project his voice in hearing distance of his friends).

Dog and Cat prance towards them. They nudge their heads in acknowledgement.

César, the soccer ball: What are you doing among them?

Dog: Why? Basking, playing, fetching with them.

Cat: Prancing, eating, sleeping. Prancing, eating, sleeping. Prancing, eating, sleeping, (as he stretches in his feline manner.)

Moi, the beaver: Huh? How can you cavort with such creatures that's making Great Big Brother sick?

Dog: Why? Easily. They feed me. They pat me. They play with me. They even walk with me and protect me.

Cat: They feed me, as well. They pat me, as well. They let me sleep and lounge a-l-l-d-a-y-l-o-n-g.

César, the soccer ball: So, you won't help me help our Great Big Brother.

Dog: Why? Why would we do that? I am fine. Why bite the hands that feed me? We've got it going on, here, you know.

Cat: Yeah …, why would we want to mess things up for us?

Dog and Cat return to Chela, Ma and the others.

César, the soccer ball and Moi, the beaver dejectedly march away.

Melancholically and isolated, brave Moi, the beaver looks towards the horizon: What's it's going to take?

Responds valiant César, the soccer ball: Calamity.

Reading Comprehension

Guided Questions:

1. What was the conflict?

2. Who was the protagonist? Why?

3. Who was the antagonist(s)? Why?

4. Was there a re/solution? Why or why not?

5. How can you resolve it?

6. Who might have been the character speaking in the first person?

7. What situation or event in your life do you have in common with (the behaviors of) the flowers?

8. What situation or event in your life do you have in common with (the behaviors of) the bears?

9. What situation or event in your life do you have in common with (the behaviors of) the dog and the cat?

10. How might your personal growth differ from theirs? Use comparative words such as: whereas, while, but, in the meantime, etc. See starter examples:

11. Whereas the flowers might have shown vanity in deference to Great Brother's suffering, I _____

12. While the bears enjoyed their playtime knowing that Great Brother was suffering, I _____

13. Dog and Cat reaped immediate benefits from Ma, while Great Brother suffered, but I _____

Environmental Science

Scientific Method

Scenario 1:

British Petroleum spills crude oil in the ocean. Many bird and aquatic animals are in danger. Your job is to remove the crude oil. How might you proceed? Use the five steps of the scientific method.

Materials:
Dirty oil (used frying oil or oil from your neighborhood mechanic)
Saw dust or pencil shavings
Pie pans, or discarded pans
Cotton
Water

Procedure:
In aluminum pie pans or any discarded pans, pour in some water. (This represents the ocean.)
To the pans, add dirty oil. (This represents the spilled crude oil).
For fun, add plastic ducks, boats, and toys of your choosing.
Using the cotton swab or cotton balls, pat the oil from the ocean.
Using the saw dust or pencil shaving, sprinkle unto the spilled oil.

Hypothesis:
I think the (cotton, saw dust) works better because:

Theory:
The (cotton, saw dust) was more effective in cleaning up oil spill because:

Diagram:

Conclusion:
I learned that …

Children's Theatre

Use the following organizational chart to divide class or campers into collaborative groups.

Characters/ Actors	Set Designers set up/take down	Costume & Props	Invitations & Programs & Tech	Refreshment & Snacks
N				
César				
Moi				
F1				
F2				
B1				
B2				
B3				
B4				
Ma				
Dog				
Cat				

I. Characters:

Narrator
César the soccer ball
Moi, the beaver
Flower 1
Flower 2
Bear 1
Bear 2
Bear 3
Bear 4
Ma (nonspeaking part)
Dog
Cat

II. Set Designer: brainstorm items to bring to design a rainforest, which is the main scene; enlist donations from local businesses; reuse, recycle and remake discarded items.

III. Set up and take down: set up the scenes for dress/rehearsals/performance; take down and remove props; clean up.

IV. Invitation to parents and guests: prepare and email invitations.

V. Snacks and refreshments: establish a menu; enlist local grocers and small businesses for help and contributions

VI. Technology: Record and publish the performance on your favorite platform. Please hashtag.

#ChildrensTheatreABeaver'sRiverGoesSoccerBall
#MicheleJeanmarie
#EnvironmentalScience
#ScienceOutdoor
#NameofOrganization

Theology

I.

What is a virtue?

Define compassion.
Define self-reliance.
Define perseverance.

In "A Beaver's River Goes Soccer Ball," we learn about three virtues specifically. Make a chart like the one below. Sort the characters under the heading that best describes each. In other words, which characters exhibited compassion; which characters exhibited self-reliance; which characters exhibited perseverance?

Compassion	Self-reliance	Perseverance

II.

Write three short paragraphs making sure to include a topic sentence that defines each virtue. Cite examples.

III.

Psalm 24:1
Locate and copy here:
Where would you place the book of Psalm? (Beginning, middle or end of the Bible)

Genesis 1:26
Locate and copy here.
Where would you place the book of Genesis? (Beginning, middle or end of the Bible)

Printed in the United States
by Baker & Taylor Publisher Services